SEASONAL CRAFTS

EMILY KINGTON

When making the crafts in this book, use a table cloth, cardboard or newspaper to protect surfaces!

SAFETY FIRST

. Some plants may sting or prick you, so ask an adult before touching.
. When using scissors and glue you may need help from an adult.

CARING FOR THE ENVIRONMENT

• Never go exploring on a scavenger or nature hunt without an adult.

• Do not disturb or damage nature during a hunt.

• Try to avoid picking nature finds from trees and plants, mainly use things found on the ground.

Watch out for this sign accompanying some of the craft instructions. You may need help from an adult with these tasks.

 EASY

 MEDIUM

 HARDER

These icons are a guide to the difficulty level of each craft. They show you when you may need another pair of hands.

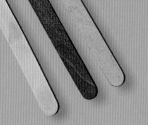

CONTENTS

SEASONAL CRAFTS

Each season brings lots of new and exciting things to discover in nature! Seasonal Crafts uses a mix of nature finds, recycled materials and craft box staples to make brilliant crafts inspired by each of the seasons. There are lots of ideas to help you be creative all year round!

The great thing about using nature finds and recycled materials is that they can be used in more than one project throughout the year, and it is all for free.

WE ARE GOING ON A SCAVENGER HUNT!

Whatever the season, there's so much to be found in nature. Head out into the great outdoors to collect some beautiful nature finds to use in your crafts. Look for flowers, leaves, sticks, seeds, and much more! Remember to take a bag with you to carry all your finds.

ABOUT SEASONAL CRAFTS

The following pages are packed with inspiring ideas for crafts to make in each season. You can follow them exactly, or make them your own by using different nature finds.

MATERIALS

Nature scavenger hunts are great for any season. Keep your eyes peeled for some interesting finds around where you live. Here is everything that was used to make all of the crafts in this book!

HOUSEHOLD AND RECYCLED MATERIALS

- An old sock
- Cardboard tubes and paper rolls
- Cereal box (or similar)
- Clothespins
- Comic magazine
- Corrugated cardboard
- Disposable dishcloth
- Fabric softener
- Flour
- Garden flowerpots
- Garden twine
- Kitchen sponges
- Large recycled lid (or baking tray)
- Paper cups
- Photographs
- Plastic lid
- Polystyrene packaging
- Popcorn bucket
- Potato
- Recycled beverage carton
- Recycled food container
- Recycled plastic bottle and lid
- Resealable food bags
- Strong cardboard box (like a shoebox)
- Stuffing from an old pillow or toy
- T-shirt
- Treats

TOOLS AND CRAFT MATERIALS

- Assorted paper
- Balloon
- Battery-operated mini lights
- Beads
- Cardstock/card
- Cookie cutters
- Cotton balls
- Craft sticks
- Double-sided tape
- Felt
- Flour
- Foam craft sheet
- Glue brush
- Glue pot
- Hole punch
- Magnets
- Masking tape
- Mini clothespins
- Mixing bowl
- Mixing spoon
- Paint
- Paintbrush
- Pair of scissors
- Pens/pencil
- Pipe cleaners
- Plastic eyes
- Pom poms (mini)
- Ruler
- School glue (PVA)
- String
- Strong glue
- Tissue paper
- Tracing paper
- Wooden skewer
- Wooden toothpicks
- Yarn

Here are some
ideas for your
own nature finds:

Acorn tops

Dried grass, seed
tops and catkins

Moss

Dried
seedpods

Leaves

Pine cones

Sticks/twigs

Chestnuts
(conkers)

Pieces of wood

Walnut
Shells

Flowers

Flower
seeds

Bamboo

Soil

Ivy

Seaweed

FLOWER PRESS FUN

Use books to make this simple flower press. It is fun and easy for anyone to do.

YOU WILL NEED:

- Resealable food bag
- Paper
- Tissue paper (optional)

TOOLS:
- School glue (PVA)
- Heavy books
- Pair of scissors

1. Spring is a great time to collect flowers to press, so it is the ideal time to go on a nature hunt.

2. Fold a sheet of paper in half (if you have tissue paper, first line the inside with it).

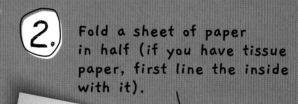

TOP TIP:
Bring a resealable bag to put them in and keep them fresh.

Tissue paper helps the flowers to dry, but remove it after two days and press the flowers directly between the folded paper.

3. Arrange your flowers and leaves on the paper, leaving plenty of space between them.

To press, put them inside the pages of a heavy book and then put more heavy books on top.

TOP TIP:
For chunky flowers arrange them face down for the best results.

4. You should press flowers and grasses for two weeks. Try not to peek at them before then.

Add paper in between your book pages to avoid staining the book.

TOP TIP:
If you gently paint your pressed flowers with school glue, it will keep them looking great for longer.

You can use pressed flowers in all kinds of crafts, so keep pressing all year round!

SOWING SEEDS IN SPRING

Planting seeds in spring will give you plenty of flowers to press all summer long!

YOU WILL NEED:

- Soil
- Flour (any kind will do)
- Packets of seeds
- Water

TOOLS:

- Large recycled lid or baking tray
- Mixing spoon
- Mixing bowl

1. Measure 10 parts of soil to 1 part of flour and mix them together.

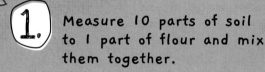

2. Slowly add small amounts of water until the mixture comes together like a dough.

3. Using your hands, roll the soil mixture into small balls.

4. Open your seed packets and sprinkle the seeds onto the recycled lid or baking tray.

5. Roll the soil balls into the seeds and let dry for three days. Toss them into your yard or garden and then wait for some beautiful summer surprises.

LOVE IN A MIST
MISS JEKYLL

If you don't have a yard/garden, you can plant seeds in flowerpots, which you can paint, too!

HAPPY ANIMAL MAGNETS

Many animals are out and about in spring. These magnets are fun to make and useful, too!

1. Trim polystyrene into a round body and make a small mount for the head.

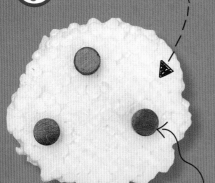

BODY

SMALL HEAD MOUNT

Glue some magnets onto the back of the polystyrene body.

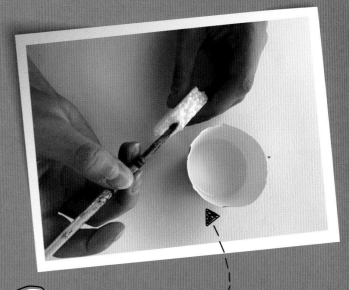

2. Seal the polystyrene mounts by painting them with school glue. This will stop the polystyrene from breaking up.

3. Make some pipe cleaner legs for the ram. The two front legs should be slightly longer than the back legs.

BACK LEGS

FRONT LEGS

Glue mini pom poms to the ends to make feet.

4. Push the legs into the polystyrene (there is no need to glue).

5. Cut the head out of cardstock/card and mount it onto the smaller piece of polystyrene.

Add plastic eyes.

One magnet is never enough! Make a rabbit using the same technique.

Push curly horns, made from pipe cleaners into the head mount.

Add stuffing to make them look fluffy!

Use string to create whiskers!

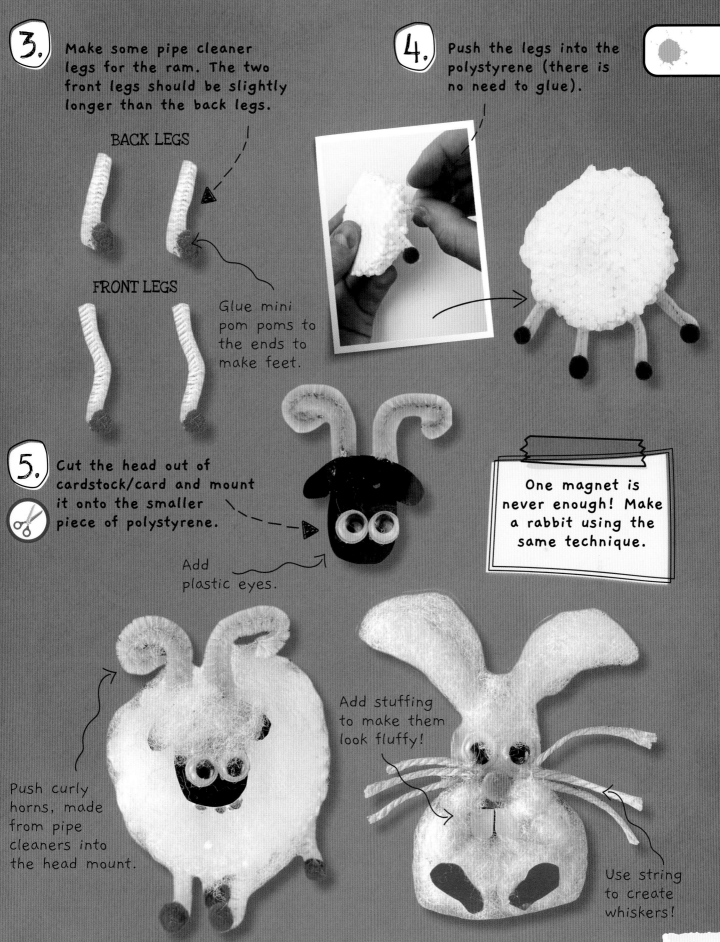

BUZZY BEEHIVE

Did you know a busy bumblebee can visit up to 6,000 flowers on a sunny day?

YOU WILL NEED:

- Yellow, black, and beige pipe cleaners
- Plastic eyes
- Tracing paper
- Cardboard box
- Felt
- String

TOOLS:
- Paintbrush/pens
- Pencil
- Paint
- Pair of scissors
- Strong glue

1. To make a bumblebee, make rings out of pipe cleaners. Wrap a pipe cleaner around a paintbrush or pen, twist it around itself, and trim off the end.

Use a smaller brush/pen to make two small rings for each end.

Make five rings, alternating between black and yellow.

Glue on the face and big plastic eyes.

Tiny face molded from pipe cleaner.

SMALL

LARGE

2. Slip the rings off and glue them all together at the twisted end.

3. Make the antennae by trimming the fluffy surface from a black pipe cleaner and mold it into shape, then glue them between the eyes.

14

4. Fold a piece of tracing paper in half. Draw half of the bumblebee wing shape along the folded edge.

BUMBLEBEE WINGS

HONEYBEE WINGS

✂ Cut out and unfold the tracing paper wings. Then draw on veins with a pencil.

✂ Cut out this shape to make two honeybee wings.

6. Glue the wings in among the rings.

5. A honeybee has a thinner body than a bumblebee, so use smaller brushes/pens to make the rings for its body.

HONEYBEE

Make three honeybees. Then glue each of your bees onto pipe cleaners like this.

7. Cut out the shape of a hive from a cardboard box.

Keep the top flap of the box to use as part of the stand.

8. Add another piece of cardboard to the back of the hive so it stands up. Glue at the top and the bottom.

Paint the hive yellow.

Fold at the dotted lines.

9. Glue string onto the hive and make some black felt doors to glue in between the string sections.

Did you know, a honeybee produces about a teaspoon of honey in their lifetime and they have FIVE eyes!

Glue your bees around the hive.

You can decorate your hive with dried flowers from your flower press (see pages 8-9).

FLOWERPOT SCARECROW

Scarecrows are supposed to scare birds away from crops. This one is too cute for that, but it is fun to have around.

YOU WILL NEED:

- Garden twine
- String
- 1 stick
- Sponge
- Moss
- Bead (or similar)
- Plastic eyes

- Felt
- Pipe cleaner
- Wooden skewer

TOOLS:

- Strong glue
- Pair of scissors

1. Fray some garden twine to glue to the end of the arms.

2. For the arms, find a stick that has a curve similar to this one.

3. Glue the frayed twine to each end of the arms. Wrap string around the stick to make it look like a striped sweater.

4. Cut a circular shape from a large sponge about the size of a table tennis ball.

5. Wrap the twine around the sponge as shown, crossing over the middle each time. Doing this will build the shape of a face. Cover the sponge completely.

6. Cut a triangle shape out of the sponge to make a hat that fits the head.

Tie some string around part of the sponge to make it look like a hat as shown.

7. Glue some moss on top of the head for the hair.

Glue the hat to the moss.

Add plastic eyes, a bead (or something similar) for the nose, and a small piece of pipe cleaner for the mouth.

8. Attach the back of the head to a long wooden skewer, using strong glue.

Then glue on the arms just below the head.

9. To make a coat for your scarecrow, cut out two felt rectangles the right length for your scarecrow's body.

Cut a hole in each piece, about a third of the way down.

10. Put the arms of the scarecrow through the holes in the felt.

Wrap the felt around the scarecrow's middle and tie with twine for the belt.

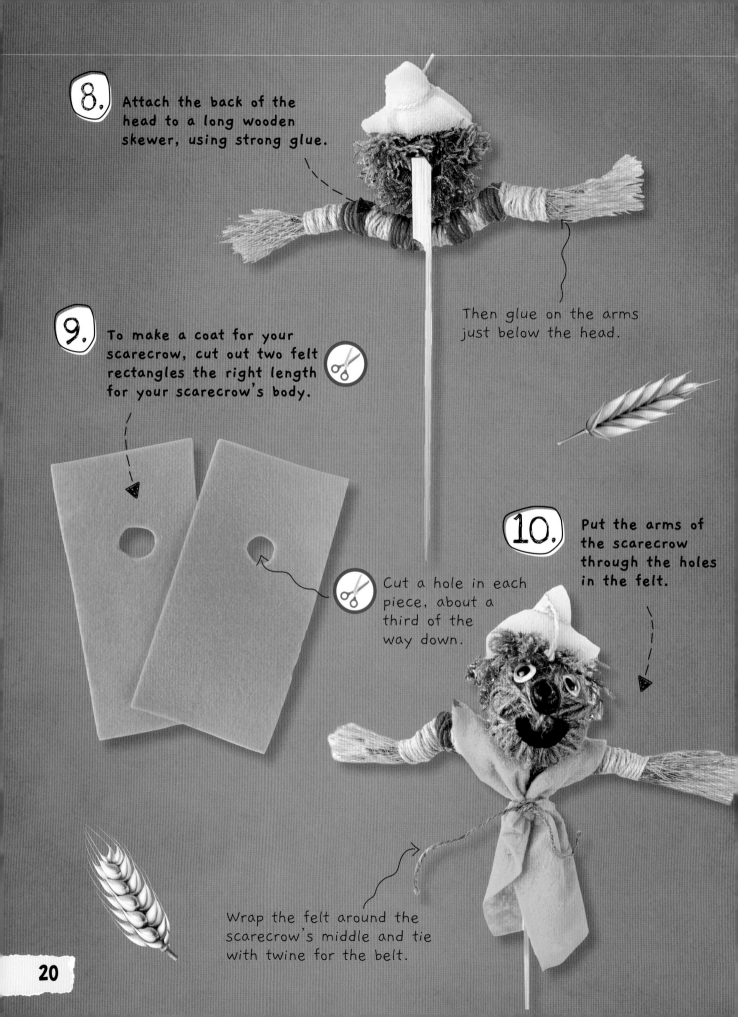

Stick your scarecrow into a flowerpot.

LUCKY CLUCKING PUPPETS

It's the chick and chicken show! These homemade puppets are a lot of fun to make.

1. To make puppets that will fit your hand, fold a piece of felt in half and draw around your hand, as shown.

2. Glue around the sides and top of the felt to join the pieces together. Do not glue the bottom, because this is where your hand goes in.

Then draw an arch shape bigger than your hand.

Cut around the arch shape to make the front and back of your puppet (two pieces of arch-shaped felt).

3. Wait until the glue is completely dry and then turn it inside out.

4. Cut out eyes and wings from felt and glue them into place. Glue on stuffing for a fluffy belly.

Twist a pipe cleaner into a cone shape for the beak.

Pipe cleaners make great feet. Glue them onto the felt.

Get creative with different features and shapes to make all kinds of cool clucking characters.

Add droopy eyelids for a sleepy look.

RAINY DAY PRINTING

Spring has sunny days, but also rainy days. This smart printing craft will keep the rainy day blues away!

YOU WILL NEED:

- Thick cardboard tube (from plastic wrap or similar)
- Assorted foam craft sheets
- Acrylic paints
- Craft paper
- Mini clothespins
- Wooden skewer

- Pressed flowers (see page 8-9)

TOOLS:
- Pair of scissors
- School glue (PVA)
- Paintbrush

1. Brush a coat of paint over a sheet of foam. This is white paint on red foam.

2. Starting in the top left corner, place the end of the tube on the painted foam. Drag it down and lift it off the surface to make a tubular pattern. Repeat until you reach the end of the sheet.

Don't worry if you make a mistake. You can paint over it and start again.

3. With clean hands, carefully lay the painted side of the foam down onto your craft paper. Press it down.

Carefully peel the foam back and let both the reverse print on paper and the foam sheet dry.

This is blue paint on a blue foam sheet.

4. Do more reverse prints using different combinations of foam sheets and paint. Keep both the reverse prints and the foam to use as backgrounds!

5. You can use the reverse print in different ways. Cut out some circular disks to use for making a collage.

6. You can also use dried flowers as a feature for your collage.

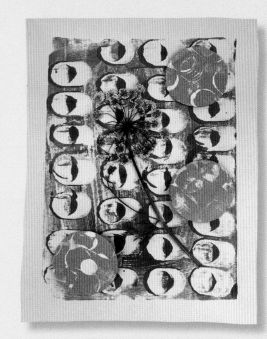

TOP TIP:
Play around with the design before you glue everything down.

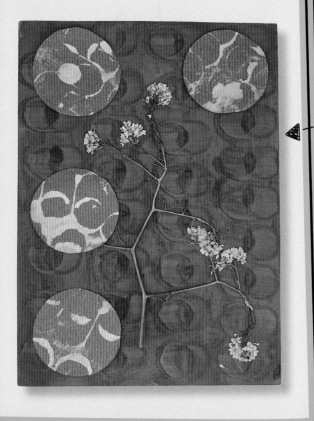

7. Glue your collage pieces down.

TOP TIP:
Use both your reverse printed papers and the foam sheets to see what different effects you get!

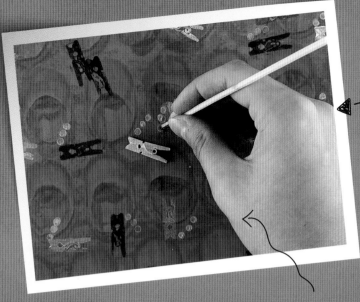

8. Create different prints using both craft and nature finds.

Add bubbles by dipping the flat end of a skewer or something similar into bright blue paint and dot it onto the foam.

Mini clothespins make great transfer prints of robotic fish against the tubular background.

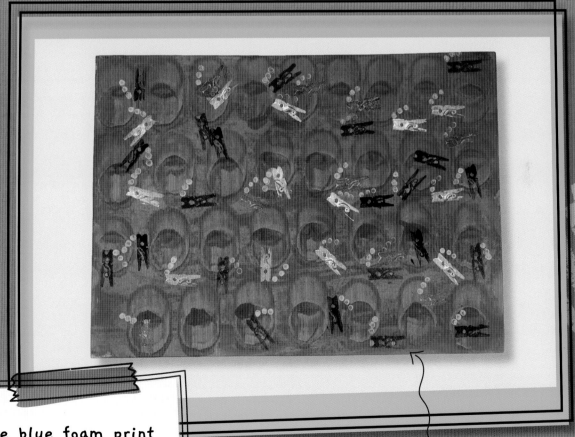

The blue foam print is great for creating an underwater scene!

Use the same clothespin over and over again. Just repaint it with different paints and press it onto the foam.

CATCH-AND-SPLASH WATER BOMBS

Make the perfect summer party game, where you will need all of your skills to stay dry!

1. Use the lid of a jar to draw a circle on a foam sponge.

2. Cut out six sponge circles, all the same size.

3. Cut three notches out of each circle at equal distances. Use the first one as a template for the other five so they are all the same.

28

4. Pierce a hole through the middle of each piece of sponge, using a skewer.

TOP TIP:
You may need help from an adult for these steps as they are difficult.

1.

Use the skewer to push through a piece of string about 8 inches (20 cm) long through the hole, as shown.

2.

5. Keep going until you have threaded all six disks of sponge onto the string.

6. Tie a knot at one end of the string. You may have to tie several knots in the same place to make sure it is big enough to stay in place.

Ask an adult to help you with this step!

7. At the other end, squash down the sponge, making it as flat as possible, and tie knots in the string to secure it.

Make as many water bombs as you like for your game!

The closer you knot the string to the sponge, the rounder your water bomb will look.

8. Decorate and strengthen a large popcorn bucket by winding string around it, gluing it down as you work.

Now it's time to play the game! Soak the water bombs before throwing them.

One person holds the bucket above their head, while another tries to throw a water bomb inside it.

You get three tries, then swap positions. There are 10 points if you get it in!

Be gentle and do not aim for people's faces.

SNAPPY SHARK TREAT BOX

Sneak your treats into the shark's mouth. It is such a cool place to hide them!

YOU WILL NEED:

- Cereal box (or similar)
- Assorted paper
- Black felt
- Pipe cleaners
- Thin kitchen sponge
- Paint (optional)
- String
- Treats

TOOLS:
- Paintbrushes
- Pair of scissors
- School glue (PVA)
- Hole punch

1. Cover the cereal box with blue paper (or paint), leaving the top flap open for now.

2. Using the front of the box to measure the correct width, draw and cut out a shape for the shark's head (A) from lighter blue paper.

Ⓐ SHARK HEAD

Ⓑ SHARK JAW

Then cut out a curved jaw (B), as shown.

3. Cut out a smaller curved mouth from black felt, as well as white paper teeth to glue onto the blue jaw.

Make a hole using a hole punch.

Attach it to the shark jaw (B).

1 inch (2.5 cm)

Fold back to make a flap.

4. Glue both the shark head (A) and jaw (B) onto the front of the box, as shown.

5. Ask an adult to cut into the box around the shark's jaw, down to the flap, to make an opening.

A

B

6. Thread a piece of string through the hole and secure on the inside of (B) with strong glue or tape.

Don't cut below the fold line of the jaw.

Make a loop at the end of the string, as shown. Pull on it to open the mouth.

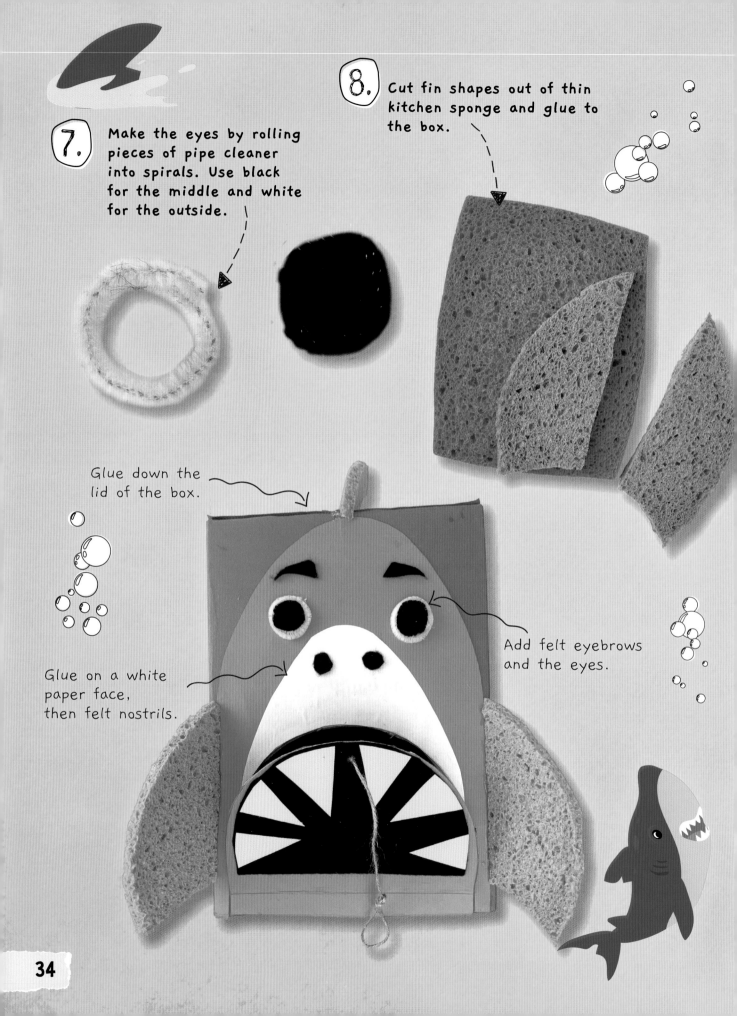

7. Make the eyes by rolling pieces of pipe cleaner into spirals. Use black for the middle and white for the outside.

8. Cut fin shapes out of thin kitchen sponge and glue to the box.

Glue down the lid of the box.

Add felt eyebrows and the eyes.

Glue on a white paper face, then felt nostrils.

Decorate your shark box with paper fish and painted bubbles. Don't forget to add the treats!

FUN T-SHIRT PRINTING

If you have an old, plain white T-shirt that is boring, turn it into a summer sensation in a few easy steps!

YOU WILL NEED:

- A clean plain T-shirt
- Acrylic paints
- Fabric softener
- Water
- Recycled jars/ paper cups (to mix paints in)
- Kitchen sponge
- Smiley face sponge (optional)
- Potato slices

- Cookie cutters
- Clothespins
- Wooden skewer
- Round acorn tops (or similar)

TOOLS:
- Paintbrushes
- Cardboard

1. Get everything ready before you start. You can first plan your design on paper.

Skewer to paint small dots.

Use cookie cutters to cut out shapes from the sliced potato. Pat the shapes dry with paper towels.

Cut out some shapes from a kitchen sponge.

Ask an adult to help you slice the potato for printing.

Acorn tops to print circles.

Recycled jar for paint dipping.

Smiley face sponge from a thrift store.

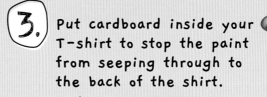

2. Mix each paint with an equal amount of fabric softener and add a dash of water.

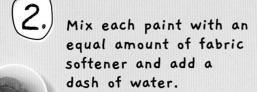

3. Put cardboard inside your T-shirt to stop the paint from seeping through to the back of the shirt.

Clothespins help to keep it in place.

Leave stamps in place to let the paint transfer.

4. Paint your stamps with a brush and carefully place them onto the T-shirt. Press down and let sit for a minute before removing.

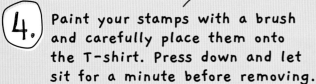

TOP TIP:
Wash your T-shirts by hand or in a separate wash and let dry naturally in the air.

HUNGRY CATERPILLAR

Most people have a few lonely socks that are no longer a pair. Use an odd sock to make a hungry caterpillar!

1. Find an old or odd sock that you no longer want.

2. Make a long tubelike shape by pushing stuffing into the sock.

3. To create the caterpillar's body, tie pieces of string tightly around equally spaced sections of the stuffed sock.

38

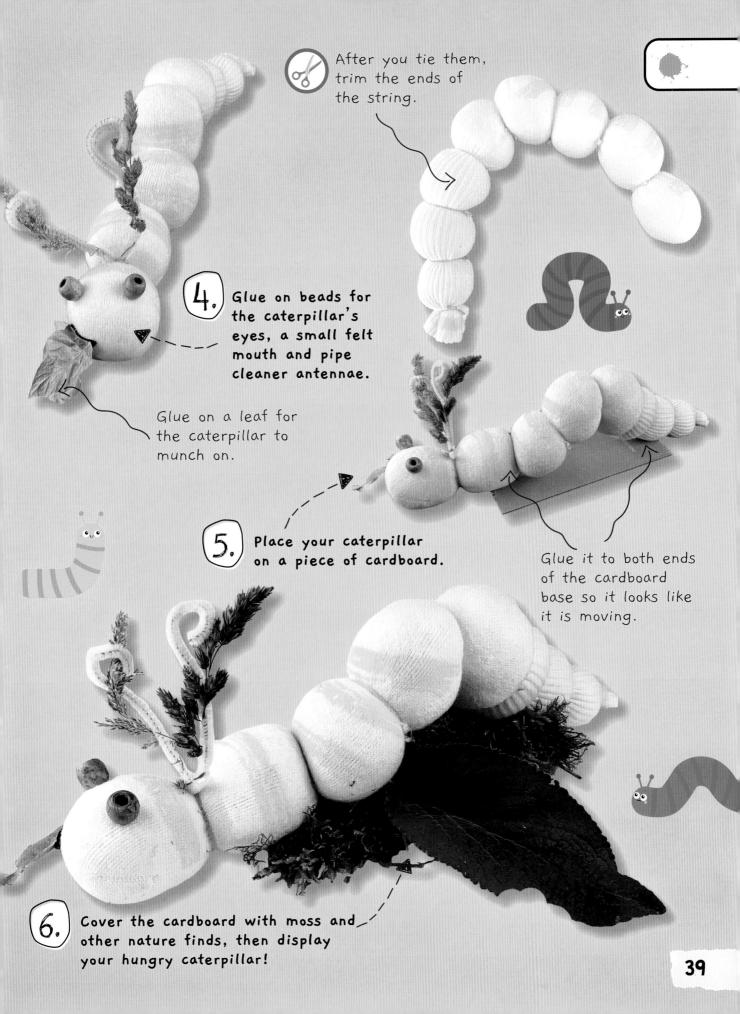

After you tie them, trim the ends of the string.

4. Glue on beads for the caterpillar's eyes, a small felt mouth and pipe cleaner antennae.

Glue on a leaf for the caterpillar to munch on.

5. Place your caterpillar on a piece of cardboard.

Glue it to both ends of the cardboard base so it looks like it is moving.

6. Cover the cardboard with moss and other nature finds, then display your hungry caterpillar!

BUG HOTEL

You will need a lot of your seasonal scavenger hunt finds to make this totally luxurious hotel for bugs and bees.

1. Some flowerpots have slits around their edge. If yours don't, use a hole punch to make holes in them so you can tie them together.

2. Tie two flowerpots together lying on their sides. Secure a flowerpot on top by threading twine through a punched hole and tying it around the twine holding the bottom two together.

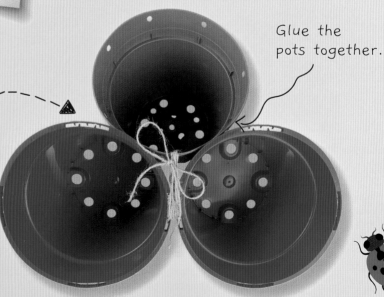

Glue the pots together.

3. Stack nature finds tightly inside each flowerpot.

Bamboo is ideal. This came from a thrift shop.

Walnut shells provide structure.

Small stones are great for little insects to hide under.

Twigs and wood can be stacked and fitted into any gaps.

Acorn tops make tiny homes.

Go back and check on it regularly to see who has checked in, but do not disturb them!

Dry moss is soft and cozy for bugs to hide in.

Add pine cones. These make a great place to stay.

FUNKY FISH MOBILE

Make this fun fish mobile to hang by your window to celebrate summer.

YOU WILL NEED:

- Cardboard
- Beads (optional)
- Nature finds
- String
- 2 long sticks
- 2 pipe cleaners
- Plastic eyes (optional)

TOOLS:

- Pair of scissors
- Wooden skewer
- School glue (PVA)
- Pen
- Acrylic paint
- Paintbrush

1. Draw a fish to use as a template for your design.

Make two of everything, because the fish will be double sided.

2. Cut out pieces of stiff cardboard to create your fish. You need separate parts for the eyes, mouth, fins, and body.

Use craft and nature finds to decorate the fish.

3. Paint your cardboard pieces. Use bright paints to make them stand out.

4. Glue the different parts of your fish onto the body using school glue.

5. Make a hole in the top of the fish using a skewer, thread string through the hole, and secure with a knot.

Make different kinds of fish using a similar method.

6. Find two sticks, about 12 inches (30 cm) long. Decorate by wrapping string around them or painting them.

7. Attach the sticks together by wrapping string or a pipe cleaner around the middle, as shown.

8. Cut four pieces of string the same length, 10 inches (12.5 cm) long, and tie one to the end of each stick.

9. Gather the four ends together and make a knot with a loop.

Attach the fish along the two sticks, arranging them at different heights.

Play around with the position of the fish until your mobile is balanced and looks great.

Different lengths of string are used for each fish.

SPOOKY SPIDERWEB DOOR SIGN

If you're busy and don't want to be disturbed, creepy-crawlies are perfect for keeping out pesky family members!

1. Use the three main sticks to make a spiderweb frame.

Tie them together using string or a pipe cleaner wrapped around the middle, as shown here.

2. Start by gluing the smallest sticks in between the gaps nearest the middle (use a strong glue).

3. Continue working out from the middle, trimming the sticks to fit the gaps as you work. Wrap string around the joints to make the spiderweb strong.

Add plastic eyes.

4. For each spider, glue pipe cleaner legs onto the bottom of a chestnut (or a ball of air-dry clay).

5. Glue the spiders onto the spiderweb.

BEWARE! KEEP OUT!

Make a sign out of cardstock/card or cardboard and glue it onto the spiderweb.

HALLOWEEN PUMPKIN LIGHTS

Pumpkin lights are amazing. Take them trick-or-treating or make a spooky window display for Halloween.

YOU WILL NEED:

- Orange string
- Balloon
- Felt (black and green)
- Pipe cleaner
- Plastic eyes
- Mini battery-operated lights

TOOLS:
- Dilluted school glue (2 parts water to 1 part glue)
- Paintbrush
- Pair of scissors

1. Mix the glue with water and partly inflate the balloon so it is still squashy.

2. Unravel a length of string and dip it into the glue mixture. Begin to wrap it around the balloon.

3. Continue to wrap the glue-dipped string around the balloon. Change directions and leave small gaps so light can shine through.

4. Leave about a ³/₄-inch (2-cm) circular gap uncovered around the knotted end of the balloon. It will become the hole needed to insert the lights.

Keep wrapping the string around the balloon until you can only see small gaps. The more layers you do, the stronger it will be.

5. When you are finished wrapping the balloon, let it completely dry overnight.

6. Pop the balloon and remove it through the gap.

7. Cut these shapes from felt to create a hat/stem and the mouth.

Make a little slit in the middle with a pair of scissors.

8. Push the pipe cleaner through the slit you made, as shown below.

9. Slip the pipe cleaner through the top of the pumpkin (with the hole on the bottom). Glue it down so it stays in place.

Slip in the battery-operated lights to make the pumpkin glow!

Add plastic eyes.

Glue on the mouth shape.

TOP TIP:
Do not put candles inside the pumpkin or leave lights in them unattended, to avoid fires.

PINE CONE OWL

This wide-eyed owl is really fun to make and uses all kinds of nature finds.

YOU WILL NEED:

- Large pine cone
- Twigs and ivy
- Pine needles (or similar)
- Dried grass and seed tops
- 2 acorn tops
- Stuffing from an old pillow or toy
- Plastic eyes
- Paper cup

TOOLS:
- Paintbrush or craft stick
- Paint
- School glue (PVA)

1. Glue dried grass onto the pine cone to create two big fluffy circles around where the eyes will be.

2. Push the white stuffing into the gaps in the pine cone.

3. Glue spiky pine needles (or similar) onto the top of the head.

Break off a section of a pine cone and glue it on, upside down, to make a great beak.

4. Glue plastic eyes onto the underside of the acorn tops, and then glue them onto the fluffy grass circles.

Make a nest for the owl.

5. Glue other nature finds around a paper cup, filling in any gaps with moss and dried grass before placing the owl into its decorated nest.

This wise old owl will look so neat sitting on your shelf!

HANGING GHOSTS

Spook up your party, or even your bedroom, with these cool hanging ghosts.

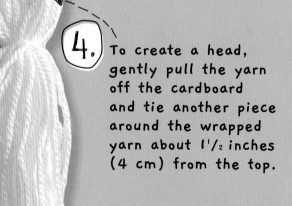

YOU WILL NEED:

- White yarn
- Orange string
- Cardboard
- Plastic eyes
- Long stick
- Ivy or other evergreen leaves/ferns
- Black yarn or felt (mouth)

TOOLS:
- School glue (PVA)
- Pair of scissors

1. Cut a piece of cardboard 6 inches (15 cm) long to wrap yarn around.

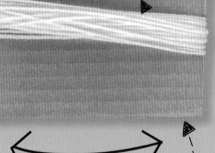

← 6 inches (15 cm) →

2. Wrap your white yarn around the width of your cardboard about 40 times.

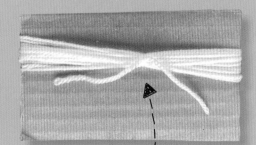

3. Cut a 5-inch (12.5-cm) length of yarn and tie it around the other strands, as shown here.

4. To create a head, gently pull the yarn off the cardboard and tie another piece around the wrapped yarn about 1½ inches (4 cm) from the top.

 Cut through the bottom of the wrapped yarn to make a tassel.

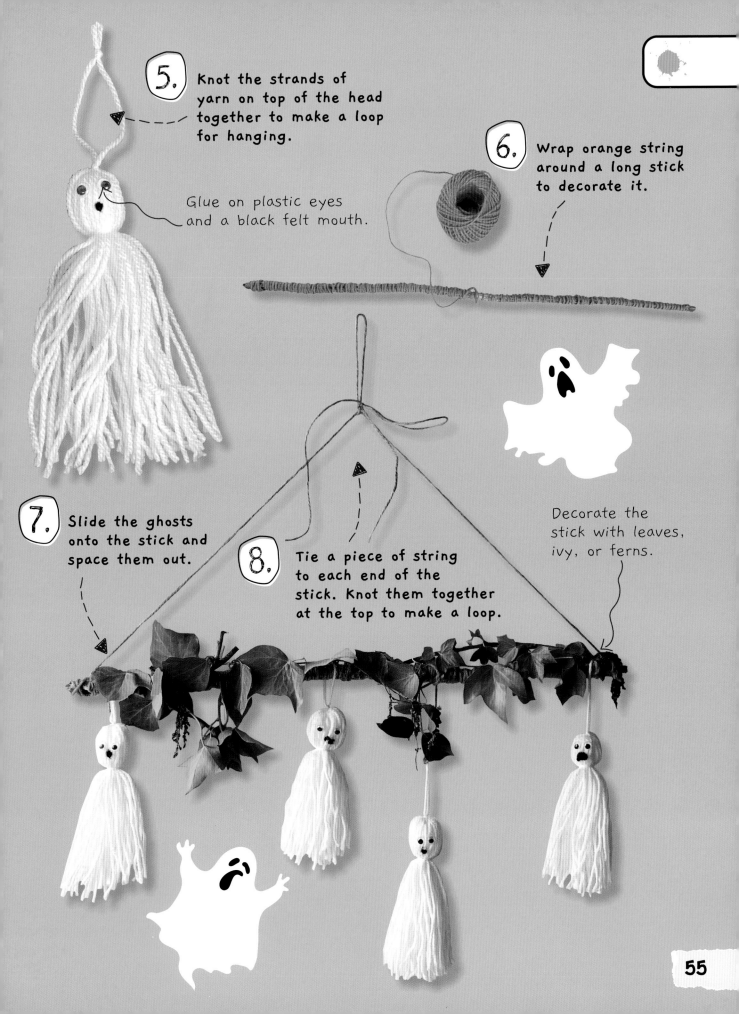

5. Knot the strands of yarn on top of the head together to make a loop for hanging.

Glue on plastic eyes and a black felt mouth.

6. Wrap orange string around a long stick to decorate it.

7. Slide the ghosts onto the stick and space them out.

8. Tie a piece of string to each end of the stick. Knot them together at the top to make a loop.

Decorate the stick with leaves, ivy, or ferns.

WOODLAND CRAFT TIDY

Bring the outside in by using woodland nature finds for this project. You will always be able to find what you need.

YOU WILL NEED:

- Strong box
- Cardboard tubes
- Paints
- Recycled food container
- Nature finds (Sticks, moss, grass, etc.)

- Felt (optional)
- Cardstock/card
- Assorted paper

TOOLS:
- School glue (PVA)
- String
- Craft sticks
- Pair of scissors

1. Use a strong box and cover it with bright paper or paint. This box was recycled from packaging.

2. For storing pens and paintbrushes, trim cardboard tubes to a height that they will fit in.

Wrap string around each cardboard tube from the top to the bottom. This makes the tube stronger, and it looks great.

Snip cuts around the bottom of the cardboard tube, and bend the tabs back so you can easily glue the bottom onto the tray.

Glue the string in place as you wrap it.

3. Decorate with a bright door made from felt and some of your nature finds.

Store stationery in here.

Acorn tops

Glue on some felt and decorate with your nature finds.

4. Wrap and glue string around a recycled food container.

There is a place
for everything,
and everything in
its place!

These dry sticks look
like old trees.

Dry moss is great to
use, because it does
not fade.

5. Make a fence with craft sticks to decorate your box. It makes a great divider inside the tray, to store craft tools.

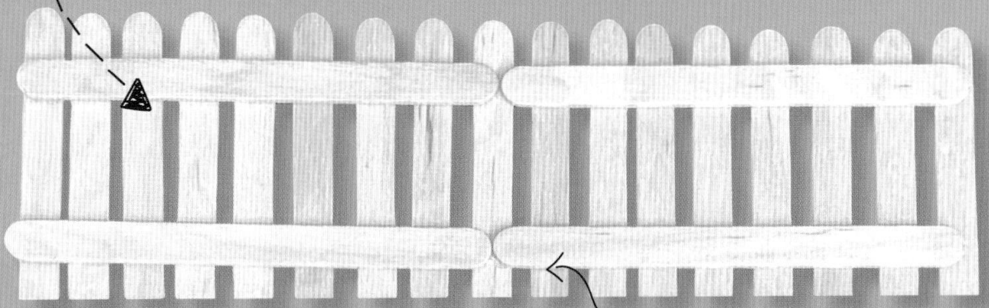

Cut the craft sticks to 3 inches (7.5 cm) long and glue them vertically along four horizontal craft sticks, as shown above.

Decorating the front of the box with a fence, and a red door makes it look cool!

THANKSGIVING LEAF GARLAND

This awesome Thanksgiving garland makes a perfect table decoration, or you can add string to hang it on a door.

1. Wind two pipe cleaners around each other to make a strong frame.

2. Make a circle by twisting the ends together, as shown.

3. Cut out a lot of small and large leaves from felt.

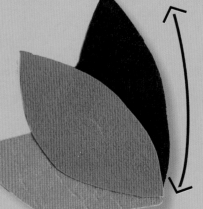

LARGE
4 inches
(10 cm)

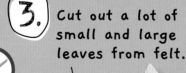

SMALL
2 inches (5 cm)

4. Glue the leaves onto the pipe cleaner frame, starting with the smaller, 2-inches (5-cm) leaves.

5. When the pipe cleaners are covered, create more layers of felt leaves by gluing them on top of each other.

6. If you plan to hang your garland on a door, make a loop of string and tape or glue it to the back.

7. Add a layer of larger felt leaves at the back.

Add natural leaves and dried grasses in between the layers of felt leaves.

Glue longer grasses and seed heads all around the wreath.

WALNUT REINDEER ON SKIS

Make a team of walnut reindeer speeding down a ski slope!

YOU WILL NEED:

REINDEER:
- 3 Craft sticks
- 6 Plastic eyes
- Felt (brown)
- 3 Mini pom poms (for the nose)
- 3 Walnut shells
- Pipe cleaners
- Twigs

SKI SLOPE:
- Twigs
- Cardboard
- Stuffing from an old pillow or toy

TOOLS:
- Strong glue
- Pair of scissors

1. Cut two antler shapes out of felt (or use small twigs) and attach with glue to the top of a walnut shell.

Glue on a pom pom nose and plastic eyes.

2. Trim a pipe cleaner to make the arms and glue to each side.

Fold the pipe cleaner arms over tiny twigs to make ski poles.

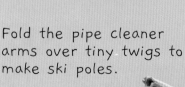

Cut a craft stick in half for the skis and glue them to the bottom of the shell.

62

3. Use cardboard for the base of the ski slope. (This is part of an old shoebox.)

Trim twigs to different sizes, from tall to short, so that they create a slope when lined up.

Glue the twigs along one side of the cardboard, from biggest to smallest, then repeat on the other side.

4. Add stuffing as snow.

These twigs make great antlers!

Reindeer love having fun on the slopes!

BRIGHT BIRD FEEDER

Winter can be a tough season for birds. Making a bird feeder is a fun and easy way to help feed the hungry birds.

YOU WILL NEED:

- Craft sticks
- String
- Sticks
- Recycled beverage carton, about 2 by 2 inches (5 x 5 cm) at the bottom
- Bird feed

TOOLS:

- Strong glue
- Pair of scissors

TOP TIP:
Measure the bottom of your carton first so you can make the feeder the right size to fit it.

1. Lay craft sticks next to each other to create a base to fit your carton.

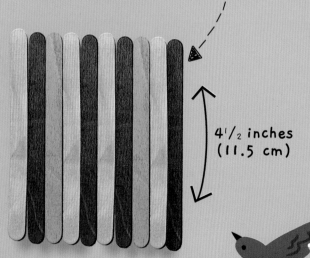

4½ inches
(11.5 cm)

2. Glue four craft sticks at even intervals across the top of your base sticks.

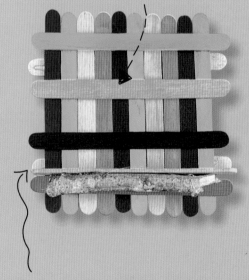

Flip it over and glue four more sticks across the other side. This makes it stronger.

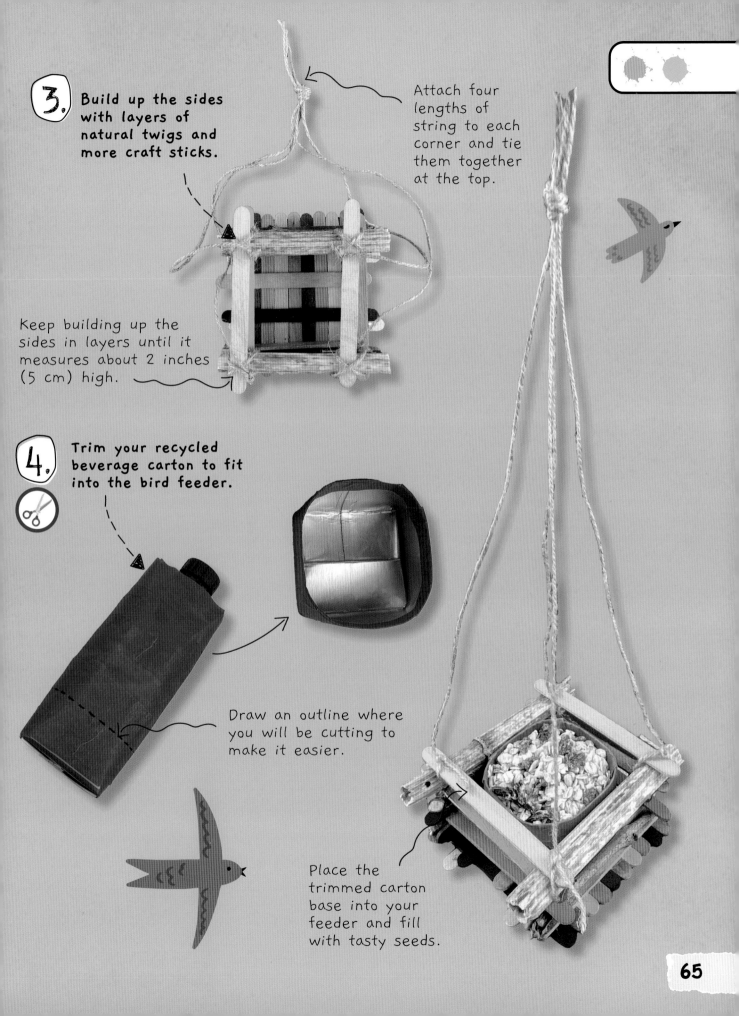

3. Build up the sides with layers of natural twigs and more craft sticks.

Attach four lengths of string to each corner and tie them together at the top.

Keep building up the sides in layers until it measures about 2 inches (5 cm) high.

4. Trim your recycled beverage carton to fit into the bird feeder.

Draw an outline where you will be cutting to make it easier.

Place the trimmed carton base into your feeder and fill with tasty seeds.

HIBERNATING BEAR

Bears hibernate during winter when food is harder to find. First they eat well, but probably not popcorn!

YOU WILL NEED:

- Garden flowerpot
- Thin kitchen sponge
- Orange and brown string
- Plastic eyes
- 8 Pipe cleaners
- Felt (ears)
- Mini pom pom (nose)
- Popcorn (for you)

TOOLS:
- School glue (PVA)
- Strong glue
- Pair of scissors

1. Find an old garden flowerpot, about 3½ inches (9 cm) in diameter. You could also use a recycled container.

2. To make the bear's head, cut out three disks from a sponge, 2 inches (5 cm) in diameter.

Wrap string tightly around the flowerpot. Glue it down as you work.

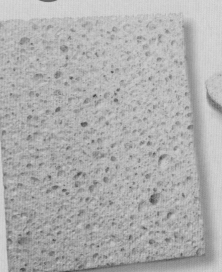

2 inches (5 cm)

3. Start to wrap the orange string around the stack of sponges.

4. Change to brown string for the last layer.

Crossing the string over in the middle as you wrap it will form the shape of the face.

Glue on a mini pom pom for the nose and the plastic eyes.

Make a mouth from felt or yarn.

Cut small oval shapes out of felt. Pinch and glue the bottom to form ears. Then glue to the bear's head.

5. Twist three pipe cleaners together. You will need two of these, one for the arms and one for the legs.

6. Wrap string around the twisted pipe cleaners to make the legs and arms.

The legs need to be bigger, so use more string than you do for the arms.

7. Add felt paws to finish it off.

Leave the end of the pipe cleaners free to attach the feet and paws.

8. Glue trimmed pieces of pipe cleaner and string onto a piece of felt in the shape of a paw. Then cut around it.

Make the feet oversized.

Twirl some string for the pad.

9. Glue the head to the edge of the flowerpot.

Glue the arms around the top of the flowerpot.

Add some string claws.

Glue the legs around the bottom of the flowerpot.

Glue on the feet.

WOODLAND WONDERLAND

Have fun creating a magical winter forest scene. It makes a great place to display treasured photos.

YOU WILL NEED:

- Assorted paper
- Cardboard
- Wooden toothpicks
- Polystyrene (from packaging)
- Wood (from a scavenger hunt)
- Mini clothespins (optional)

TOOLS:

- School glue (PVA)
- Double-sided tape
- Pair of scissors
- Pen/pencil
- Paint
- Paintbrush

1. Fold a green piece of paper into quarters.

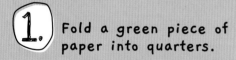

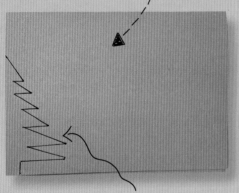

Draw half the shape of a tree along the folded side.

2. Cut along the lines and unfold to create two tree shapes. Repeat these first two steps seven times, until you have 16 tree shapes in total (to make four trees).

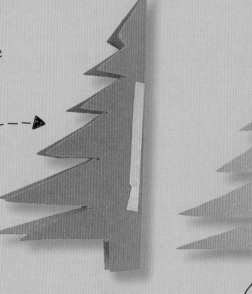

Add double-sided tape to the left of the fold line on each tree shape (or you could use glue instead).

3. Attach two tree shapes together at the fold.

4. Then stick on two more tree shapes to make a finished tree.

5. Ask an adult to help you trim the side and top flap of a cardboard box.

Draw around something round, such as a small plate, to create hill shapes along the crease of the box.

6. Cut around your shapes and cover the hills with bright paper.

7. Paint the top of your wood white. To hold everything in place, glue the wood to both the cardboard base and the hill background.

8. Cut out some simple paper leaf shapes and decorate with a pen or crayon.

Use tape to attach wooden toothpicks onto the back.

Push your leaves into the cardboard holes at the top.

Glue your trees in place.

Make some smaller trees, too!

Cover the base in school glue and break up the polystyrene and sprinkle it all over.

Use mini clothespins to attach photographs to your scene.

Make it a memory board by adding photographs of the great times you have had, including crafts you have made!

RECYCLED CARTOON SNOWMAN

Create your own seasonal character with attitude! Twist the head around to change its mood.

YOU WILL NEED:

- Paints/pens
- Cardboard tube
- Disposable dishcloth (Scarf)
- Comic magazine (optional)
- Cotton balls
- Stuffing from an old pillow or toy
- Recycled plastic bottle and lid
- Pipe cleaners
- String
- Yarn (hat)

TOOLS:

- Pair of scissors
- School glue (PVA)
- Glue pot
- Glue brush
- Masking tape

1. Cover the bottle with masking tape. It will make it easier to glue things to it.

Use a bottle with a good sized lid. It will become the head.

2. Build the snowman shape by dipping cotton balls into a pot of school glue (PVA) and attaching them in rows to the bottle.

Use a double layer around the middle of the body to get to a rounded shape.

3. Cover the body with a layer of fluffy white stuffing, and glue it in place as you work.

4. Glue cotton balls around the lid to make a round head and cover with stuffing.

Do not cover the hole at the bottom of the lid, because you need to screw it onto the body.

5. Wrap string around a pipe cleaner to make arms (see method on page 68).

Make a beanie hat for the snowman!

6. Cut lengths of yarn to about 12 inches (30 cm) long.

Fold each length of yarn in half.

7. Cut a ring from the end of a cardboard tube 1 inch (2.5 cm) wide.

Push the loop end of the folded yarn through the ring.

8. Take the two ends of the folded yarn and put it through the looped end of yarn.

Pull to get a knot.

9. Repeat this process all the way around the ring until it is completely covered.

10. Gather the loose threads to make a dome shape and tie them with a loose piece of yarn, as shown.

Trim to make a short pom pom that sticks up.

11. Cut out the eyes and mouth from a comic magazine or draw your own!

Cut a long strip of disposable dishcloth and decorate it to make a scarf.

Glue on the arms.

Glue a face on each side of the head.

TURN YOURSELF INTO AN ELF

This craft would make a great gift for a relative to display on a shelf. It's guaranteed to make them smile!

YOU WILL NEED:

- Cardboard
- Craft sticks
- Felt
- Cotton balls
- String
- Photograph of you

TOOLS:

- School glue (PVA)
- Pair of scissors
- Pencil/pen
- Strong glue

1. Draw an outline of a body. Bend the cardboard at the waist and knees.

2. Use felt to make clothes. Attach them to the cardboard with school glue.

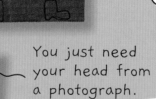

You just need your head from a photograph.

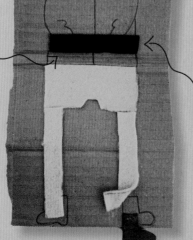

Leave a space for the glue line.

3. To make you sit upright, glue the gap between the belt and pants with strong glue.

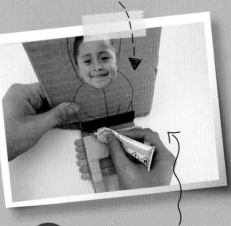

Make some boots and a belt and glue them on.

Hold it in place until the glue is completely dry.

4. Turn it over and glue craft sticks in a row to make a seat.

5. Add a felt jacket, then cut around the outline of the body.

Draw the shape of arms with a pen and add some felt gloves.

Decorate your boots with pieces of cotton ball and little bows of string.

Add a hat and scarf.

RECYCLED ART

WHAT CAN I SEE IN THE WILD?

BEETLE BOOKS

BEETLE BOOKS

Make an elf for your whole family!

INDEX

Picture Credits:
(abbreviations: t-top; b-bottom; m-middle; l-left; r-right; bg-background)

Shutterstock: Aleksandra Kirichenko 46-47 (spiderweb illustrations); alexdndz 22-23 (illustrations); anat chat 7tl;asharkyu 7mr; Benton frizer 66-69 (illustrations); Branislava R 3tr, 6bm, 27tr; Chlorphyll 47ml; Cloudystock 74-77 (illustrations); Dmitry kolmakov 3br; drawkman 12bl; El Sy 49mr, 51b; elenaforly 54-55 (illustrations); EmArts 7ml; Emily Li 4br; Good luck images 1tl, 5tr, 6tl; ilina93 7mr; imaginasty 48-51 (illustrations); ink.mousy 40-41 (illustrations); Irina Adamovich 56-59 (illustrations); Katya Kandalava 60-61 (illustrations); kichikimi 64-65 (illustrations); KN 8-9 (illustrations), 10-11 (illustrations); KsanaGraphica 32-35 (bubble illustrations); kzww 7bl; Lattersmile42-45 (illustrations); Luciafox 62-63 (illustrations); Marish 70-73 (illustrations); megapixel 2br; movatliz 78-79 (bell illustrations); Natykach Natalia 18-21 (illustrations); Nora Hachio 52-53(illustrations); Ortis 4ml; Ramona Kawlitzki 36-37 (illustrations); smart design 28-31 (illustrations); SplayTruffel 32-35 (shark illustrations); stockvit 14-17 (bee illustrations); tortila 78-79 (elf illustrations); Triff 1bl, 5ml, 6tr, 6m; Valentina Razumova 1br; Vaulomova 46mr Natalia; vectorsbang 24-27 (illustrations);Vectortatu 74-77; vvoe 2br; wisnu bayu aji 14-17 (honeycomb illustrations); world of vector 38-39 (illustrations); Zhane luk 7br.

First published in 2022 by Hungry Tomato Ltd
F15, Old Bakery Studios, Blewetts Wharf, Malpas Road, Truro, Cornwall, TRI IQH, UK

Thanks to our creative team
Senior Editor: Anna Hussey
Graphic Designer: Amy Harvey

A CIP catalogue record for this book is available from the British Library.

Beetle Books is an imprint of Hungry Tomato.

ISBN 978-1-914087-66-0

Printed and bound in China

Discover more at:
www.mybeetlebooks.com
www.hungrytomato.com